STOP THE CLOCK

The Tao of Time and Timelessness

A Field Guide for the Cosmic Warrior

STOP THE CLOCK

The Tao of Time and Timelessness

A Field Guide for the Cosmic Warrior

By John Warren Flint

DeVorss & Company, Publisher
Box 550
Marina del Rey, California 90294-0550

Contents

This Book Is Dedicated

To My Father

Introduction

Two times during my life, my father took me aside and said, "John, you will have to work your entire life so you had better find something you really enjoy doing, even though I may not agree with what it is."

That touched me deeply.

Once when I was seventeen, I drove him to the airport, and while we were traveling I asked him why he had stayed with one company for so long when other jobs available to him offered him a higher salary.

"My company never asked me to lie," he answered.

I appreciated my father more during the last six years of his life, for I learned to accept him as he was. When I was growing up, we had a stormy relationship which was never very close. I felt he did not really love me.

Later, I gained a deeper insight into his inner nature, realizing that he had always loved me; it was just that we had different ways of expressing our love for each other. My *expectations* of *how* he should love me got in the way. Naturally, when those expectations dropped away, we shared openly with one another, and got to know each other better.

As a child at Christmas-time, I would ask him what he would like most of all—he always said all he wanted was ''peace and quiet.'' At that time, I could never understand why he would want such a thing.

How much fun could you have with ''peace and quiet?''

Two months before he died of a heart attack, he took me aside and said that he wished someone had told him earlier in his life how important it was to relax.

The world shares with us in many ways—may we embrace the sharing.

CHAPTER 1

The Birth of the Cosmic Warrior

IT IS THE TIMELESSNESS for this book to be written again. We are realizing that all of the words have been written and the secrets have been spoken. I remember going into a large bookstore twelve years ago and finding only a few titles available on the "New Age" metaphysics, astrology and meditation. I used to have to go to small out-of-the-way occult bookstores to locate such writings. Now the writings are out "en masse." The fever of "spiritual voyeurism" is upon us. The texts and the therapies continue to open new doors. Yet, many are still hungry. The books and most popular therapies are all like cookbooks. They leave you with all the "right" words, insights, theories, yet you are still hungry. After a week or a year, you need the next volume or the advanced workshop.

Those are the cookbooks. They offer many promises, yet you continue to starve and the starving is worse because now you have been made aware of the so-called mysteries and secrets of your universe.

This book was written for those of you who have sincerely tried to become more aware and are still hungry. You have read Rajneesh, Ram Dass, Nathaniel Branden, Leo Buscaglia, Dr. Wayne Dyer, *Love is Letting Go of Fear*, *No Boundary*, *Handbook to Higher Consciousness*, *The Road Less Traveled*, *Winning Through Enlightenment*, *Illusions* and other New Age consciousness books. Yet, the mind wants more, just one more book.

The theme the mind always seems to chant is "it," the answer, is never where you are, what you know or what you have.

You have experienced EST, LRT, TM, A Course in Miracles, Rebirthing, Jungian Analysis, Rolfing, the Guru and other therapies, and you are still in need of one more session, another tap on the third eye, or a follow-up workshop.

Only if you have been working and searching as hard as you can, will you appreciate this book. Even knowing you need to look within is not enough. If you have not tried with all your heart you will think that what I am going to share with you is too simple to be true. You will still believe that all it takes to unlock the secrets is more hard work, effort and discipline. Until you have reached the point where you have tried everything, you are still looking for the advanced technique, volume II, the sacred mantra, or the final graduate workshop for illumination.

What I would like to do is show you how to *remember* what you have been searching for. The words that have been written and spoken by your teachers, therapists and Gurus are beautiful. They have not been wrong. But, the words fill your mind and only momentarily satisfy you. They do not feed you. The mind wants truth to be complicated; it never feels it has enough awareness to understand. The nature of the mind is to do this. Your mind is in an eternal race and it wants to know how long the race will be so it can pace itself.

Now join me as we walk along a path of remembrance together. A ''memory'' of the past is a moment of conscious awareness. When you go back into the feeling of a memory (many calendar years ago) it feels as if no time had gone by. The feeling is fresh as this moment, now. Consciousness is timelessness. Mystics say we are light. To experience higher consciousness is to move into light. Physicists say there is no time at the speed of light. Timelessness is the key to remembrance. What we must learn is to stop the clock. We must *remember* this.

I was sitting with a group of people preparing to begin a meditation class. The hostess for the meeting asked if

I wanted her to stop the pendulum clock on the wall for the meditation. I had not even heard it until she mentioned it to me. I said, "No, it will not be necessary to stop it." The group sat down and we began to quiet our minds. As I moved into the silence, the noise of the clock became louder and louder. I felt like asking the hostess to come back and stop the clock. How could we meditate with such noise going on? I had let go of noises before, but this one seemed to be after me.

Then, as I sat quietly, inwardly fighting the noise, I recognized a basic life principle at work. The clock's noise was something that I did not like. I would have preferred the room to be totally quiet; my *expectation* was that the room should have been soundless.

Further, the warrior nature within me said I should fight that which I did not like, so that it would desist. What I noticed was that the more I fought with the sound of the clock, the louder it became. In trying to control the clock, it now controlled me. At this point, physically stopping the clock would not have resolved the inner struggle that the clock (my therapist) was helping me to understand.

I tried another approach: simply embraced the clock, and its annoying sound. By breathing from the gut of my being, basic, deep diaphragmatic breathing, I let the clock be itself. The annoyance thus disappeared, and I did not hear it again until after the meditation.

The dynamics of the process I have described will be shared throughout this book as we go into the issues of control, meditation, anger, not knowing and letting go.

Certainly to say, "let go" sounds like a "right answer," but it does not get "the job" done. The dynamics of letting go manifest in your solar plexus. It may go against what you have been trained to accept as Truth. I am talking now about embracing that which you do not like, without the fear that if you stop fighting, "it" will conquer and control you. If this basic concept of control cannot be applied to your everyday life, letting go is rendered useless.

Before you go off on any metaphysical tangents concerning thoughts about the Infinite, you need to deal with *where* you are at this moment in time. . . not where you *thought* you were, or where you think you *should* be, but where you are *right now*. Where you are at this living moment is the direct path to knowing, experiencing, being.

But who are you? Who is asking the question?

The key to the experience of who is asking the question, is the key of timelessness. We are trying to control and stop the clock. In doing so, we think we will have my father's wish for his "peace and quiet." However, the mind thinks it does not (intrinsically) have this exterior thing called "peace and quiet," so the mind seeks to go out and *get* it. Thus begins the control game, which leads us away from Truth. The inner theme is to get out of your throat-and-neck-center where your breath is shallow and breathe into your solar plexus. This is the key to digestion, the timelessness of the direct experience.

We are experiencing a time of major transition in our world; the "new man" within must be born. This book is a guide for the rebirth of that being as we move into this "New Age." The Machiavellian Warrior of the past is dying and the Cosmic Warrior is being reborn. We move through our everyday lives creating images of control. If we see everything we attempt to control as *outside* of us, we split ourselves in two. That which appears outside is, in reality, reflecting what has already manifested within. We end up having that which we attempt to control, control us instead. The battle is within.

The awakening is not a birth of someone new who is separate from us. It is rather a conscious movement into that which is already there. It is the path of the child who sees everything as part of the whole. Unfortunately, he is soon taught to see differences and separations among the parts. The Cosmic Warrior is returning to that early vision of wholeness, seeing how all the unique aspects of life are a part *of*, not apart *from* the whole.

In the past, when we had a clock that needed to be stopped, we would go outside of ourselves and stop it. The problems of life, we are told, are outside us and must be taken care of through some outward action.

Therefore, the so-called Law of Cause and Effect should be seen from a new perspective, through the Law of Reflection. That which we see outside of us is no more than the reflection of where we are *at that moment*. When we are unhappy, we try to change our lives by changing the *situation*, or the *person* outside of us. We never really deal with the part of us that the person or situation was trying to show us.

I experienced a marriage where my partner was extremely judgmental. Because of my ''New Age'' beliefs, insights, and understanding, I felt I was not ''that way.'' But after continually trying to teach *her* the ''right way'' to be, my conclusion was to want to leave the relationship, saying that she was so stubborn and unaware that she would never gain higher consciousness and understanding.

During the separation and subsequent divorce, I came to an understanding. The Law of Reflection was at work. We leave a painful relationship to continue the search for a perfect one. What I saw as judgmental in my former wife was a reflection of my own nature. She may have been outwardly judgmental, but I held mine inside continually judging myself.

Our partners (our reflections) cannot change outwardly until we change inwardly. This is why we are split in two trying to enforce changes in our relationships. How difficult it is to see ourselves even in front of a mirror. After our own metamorphosis, either the partner will reflect our change or the relationship will dissolve and each will move on. Our responsibility is to understand the Law of Reflection.

Our life is like a movie. It is so good (so real) that we forget we are observing it on the screen. We get lost, we forget, we are drawn into the drama, not knowing we are in the very center of all movies we see. The birth of the Cosmic Warrior is a movement into that center of awareness. In the midst of this experience time dissolves. From the center, we move into life experiences without fear or blame, judgment or worry.

When Jesus said, "Love your enemies," he meant your so-called enemies, those who are showing you a part of you which you need to deal with and to be aware of.

Enemies, like noisy clocks, are helping us to be reborn. It is not easy being an enemy, always showing someone his dark side. We try to get rid of our enemies so that we may embrace only our friends and loved ones. We need to embrace all, for each is showing us a part of ourselves. The former marriage partner thus becomes a great teacher, a blessing.

Knowing that the world reflects where we are, and that life is a mirror, is not enough. We must *experience* it. I call this experience the process of digestion; not digesting what we have been *told* to believe, but finding out what we believe through direct experience. This was a sacred ritual of the North American Plains Indians.

They would go out into the wilderness to fast and experience their visions. Today, we are lacking this quest for inner vision in our society. Our visions and dreams have been replaced by television. When we learn to digest, we experience timelessness, the door to our vision beyond time and space. The vision we see is that which feeds us on all the paths we may walk. It is Dharma, Torah, the law internal and eternal; it is love.

TIME IS

Too Slow for those who Wait
Too Swift for those who Fear
Too Long for those who Grieve,
Too Short for those who Rejoice;
But for those who Love,
Time is not __________

—Henry Van Dyke

The Cosmic Warrior within faces the greatest of all challenges, and only through living in timelessness, he remains fully awake. The challenge, therefore, is not letting go of that which you *do not want*, but learning how to let go of that which *you want more than anything*. The full enjoyment of any of life's most pleasurable experiences is linked with one inescapable fact: it is all over too soon. Yet that which is most painful seems to drag on and on.

Time is the theme in which we are inextricably involved. The "time-space continuum" is experienced and conceptualized from the mind in the throat-and-neck-center, the source of our dualistic approach to life. From the center of our being, the solar plexus, time is not an issue. It is our natural clock which is attuned to inner and outer cycles. Struggling with time (the thought of being behind schedule, for instance), you push from your throat-and-neck-center without listening to your solar plexus, where there is no time—only being.

A further illustration is found in skiing. When you ski from your head, you experience fear, straining and exhaustion. The opposite is true when you ski from your solar plexus. Time dissolves. You are not *trying* to ski, you are not even skiing, yet you ski.

There are two "you's:" the you that you think you are, the rational mind, Ahamkara, the ego-maker, Mercury the Messenger, Hermes the Trickster, (which I call the throat-and-neck-center), and the other you that is found at your solar plexus, where you experience pure being, fully participating in whatever the world has to offer.

The Cosmic Warrior sees all that is unique as *part* of the whole. The ego, however, sees uniquenesses as separate from the *whole*, and thus further divides or divorces life into male-female, good-bad, light-dark. The ego thrives on dualities and devotes its life to mediating between these opposites seeking peace, as a result of opposites coming together. Order, control or peace that is attained externally (one that brings two opposites together into oneness) is death, lifelessness based on fear of war. Peace *within* allows two *apparent* opposites to co-exist: seen as a part of a whole, separations vanish. Female becomes *part* of male, male becomes *part* of female. Thus there is no conflict, no war, no internal-external division to separate us from that which ''is.''

The Cosmic Warrior is at peace in the midst of change. Saying that peace is not an action-external but a feeling-internal is not enough—we need to digest the Truth, take it out of the images of mind, time and space and bring it down from the throat-and-neck-center to the solar plexus, and truly live it. The mind has an *image* of peace that gets in the way of peace. The mind has an *image* of God, reality, and love that gets in the way of all that is timeless and unlimited.

Knowing what keeps us from this direct experience in the mind is not enough. That is the cookbook technique, and I am not talking about preparing the meal. I am talking about digesting the meal. That is what feeling filled (fulfilled) is all about. You can eat all day long, experience all lifetime long, and the mind will say that it is not enough. It is never enough. You are already the Cosmic Warrior; now it is time to be initiated. You must stop the clock by living in timelessness; embrace your life and all those in it. If you do not embrace it, you cannot move on. If you fight what you do not like, you feed it and it grows. Do not continue to do this. Breathe from your solar plexus, not from your throat and neck.

In the therapeutic bodywork experience of Rolfing, by fighting and tensing against the supposed pain of the body work, the pain gets worse. By embracing the pain, the pain melts away. Where was the pain? The Cosmic Warrior sees pain as a message that says that something needs attention. Pain is a message, so do not try to push it away.

Your rational mind has said there are good messages and bad messages. But I say there are just messages. We end up seeing only part of the whole and calling it One. Every dream, vision, and experience has something to say. The Cosmic Warrior is learning how to listen.

CHAPTER 2

It's OK Not to Know

THE FEAR OF NOT knowing is one of the blocks the Cosmic Warrior encounters along the path of self-realization. From birth up to about the age of four, it is OK not to know. After all, you are just a baby and not knowing is not a fearful experience. But as one enters school, the entire picture changes. The child's openness suddenly falls prey to rational calculation. The process of education inevitably involves authority figures who test the learning experience.

For the first time, not knowing is failure. Preschool children, however, live from their Buddha bellies; moving into each activity in life, they accept change. Each child lives according to his own dance, and acceptance of change is implicit in his actions. The key word here is spontaneity. So as a child, you can suck your thumb all you want, and wet your diapers and experience the feeling of wonderment. You can experience this spontaneity until you reach a certain age; then it is down to business and rules of learning and education. As the children grow older, their actions are judged by members of the adult world as either being right or wrong.

In school, the teacher's ego is on the line if the student does not learn effectively. In this way, not knowing becomes failure. Breathing from the Buddha belly stops, breath is caught up in the throat-and-neck-center. What occurs is shallow breathing—stomach in, chest out as you breathe in. Babies live in timelessness, breathing from the solar plexus. When we forget our natural way of breathing, we take shallow breaths and choke off our true self-awareness. Digestion is the process of remembering to breathe from the solar plexus (in breath—stomach out, out breath—stomach in), and it is even more important than meditation. Unless you are breathing naturally ''from the gut,'' you will be meditating to get something (i.e., satori, samadhi, cosmic consciousness, which is living in timelessness) instead of meditating because you are already living in timelessness. Trying to attain cosmic consciousness is saying that it is separate from you and not already a part of you.

In our culture, all dualities but one are supported or fed by institutions. In the area of health, ''sickness'' is supported by doctors, hospitals, pharmaceutical companies; ''well-being'' is supported by health clubs, spas, sport activities, and health food stores.

In the field of law and order, the image of the ''good guys'' is portrayed by police and FBI; outside the field of law and order, the image of the ''bad guys'' is portrayed by a network of criminals and criminal activities. Such deceptively simple dualities make up the game board of life.

However, the lone institution whose duality is not culturally supported is education/knowledge. The act or state of ''knowing'' is supported by school systems and the media, but ''not knowing,'' its opposite, is totally unaccepted. In effect, just to get on the game board itself, one must ''know'' the rules.

I would like to create an institute of Higher Not Knowing because this area needs to be embraced and supported as well. At the present moment, you know more than you knew ten years ago. You also know hardly anything compared to what you will know ten years from now. So we are all standing at this point of wanting to know, projecting our past knowledge into the so-called future in an attempt to get rid of not knowing.

Change is the nature of our life experience. Trying harder to control our lives, we end up controlled by them. We want to appear to be knowing, knowledge-able, yet our vision is limited because we cannot accept not knowing.

The Cosmic Warrior learns how to stand and face the unknown which each day brings. If we try to make everything known, life dies, loses its spontaneity. This is what happens when people become fearful; tightening up, they breathe shallowly and become as rigid as their belief systems. You cannot "talk" your mind out of fear; you have to breathe into it. Breathe free, be free. Locking into the fear brings into your life what you have feared; thus you have created your reality.

I believe our basic desire is to be *real*—to be in a *real situation* even if that reality is painful; to have something to hold on to, in spite of the pain.

> A person yells for help as he grabs on to a rose bush and finds his hand is bleeding from the thorns. When you come to help and realize why he is in pain, you tell him to let go of the rosebush. He says, "No, I won't let go of it, it is my rosebush. But, help me, I am in pain."

In dealing with the unknown, we must understand the word "faith." Growing up, I had been told to have faith, and everything would be all right. Having faith meant trusting in God and Jesus, higher powers, that which was outside of me. I fought with the word faith for a long time because it represented a passive stance, and throughout my life I had been trained for action. Many contradictions arose within me. In the midst of the battle over faith, an insight about faith was born. What happened soothed my entire being. I began to feel more comfortable facing the unknown; an understanding occurred which embraced life and its whole drama. Thus, the Cosmic Warrior was born. This meant that I did not have to *know* to feel comfortable and secure, but I could continue to *grow, unfold, remember*, without fear of failure. Faith now meant that life would only show me what I needed to see and would reveal to me that part of me I needed to understand.

Our mind's limited knowledge and understanding as well as rigid beliefs as to what spirituality and higher consciousness are, block our acceptance of not knowing. Even if I say, ''to experience your higher consciousness means living in timelessness,'' you might *know* in your mind what I am saying, but would you be *living* in time-lessness?

Embracing ''not knowing'' does not mean ''not caring'' about knowing. You care even more, not less. It is the mind which judges what caring should be. Sometimes, in order to help someone, you must say, ''I can't help you.'' Denying is therefore helping in a certain situation.

In a way, we are like plants on different ''watering schedules.'' A watering schedule may change weekly, monthly, yearly. And, unlike actual plants, with humans there is no set pattern. When you know your own cycle, you will understand the nature of cycles in others. All of this comes from your solar plexus, your true horoscope, your center of desire. Breathing from your solar plexus attunes you to your nature so you do not overwater or underwater yourself, or others. If a loved one is a cactus this week, month or year, do not feel you have to keep watering to be a ''good guy.'' If caring means giving water every day, you will tend to overwater, and kill that which you love with ''kindness.'' Your fear, in this instance, is in being called a ''bad guy.''

There is no one external rule to follow, no one single way, internal and eternal. Lao Tzu in the *Tao Te Ching* says, ''There are ways, but the way is uncharted.'' There *is* one way, not from your head as rational-mind proponents declare, but from your solar plexus, the path of timelessness. Only *you* know how painful it was when you did not listen to your gut and did what parents, teachers, friends said you should do. How many of us have gone against our inner law? When you go against what you feel, the pain seems as if it will never go away. The inner law is timeless and unchanging. The outer laws are constantly changing, never leaving us with a sense of peace.

Anarchy from the throat-and-neck-center (the ego), produces selfishness and chaos; whereas anarchy from the center of your solar plexus is peaceful and a unique part of the wholeness in which you live. We all live in timelessness, but when this part of our being is interpreted by the throat-and-neck-center, whatever we are observing is seen as eternal.

We see in our culture the institution of marriage as two people, external, man and woman, coming together forever and ever. We forget that marriage is the male and female nature within one individual coming together in a timeless experience of unity. In our culture, we take an eternal principle, such as marriage, and force it onto the earth stage of limited conceptuality, surrounded by time and space.

A church once held the opinion that after marriage there could be no divorce. A truth internal, but a hell external, in a world of constant change. Marriage is an inner experience, which we need to share in our everyday lives. The Cosmic Warrior lives in the midst of this true union, embracing the male and female within, but not neutralizing or neutering himself.

⊕⊕ is my logo and symbol of this union.

It is this marriage, this union-internal, that allows us to live in the midst of the duality, of knowing and not knowing. The union is timeless, never beginning, never ending.

CHAPTER 3

Garbage and Other Blockages to Surrendering

Yes, you must even embrace your garbage. (Some may want to use the word "shit" instead of garbage.) Start breathing from your gut. Breathe in slowly, deeply, let your stomach out as you breathe in. Breathe out, stomach in. Now, you are ready to embrace your garbage.

I see garbage as a discarded peel which protected the banana before it was eaten. Shit is no more than the left-over packaging that protected the nutrients your body needed.

Garbage and shit perform a spiritual task every bit as important as nutrient-storing. Without garbage, there would be no nutrients, but our minds have judged garbage as bad, nutrients as good. Again, to say that garbage is neither good nor bad does not mean you should eat garbage and reverse the normal process.

The judgement here of good/bad is yet another way the mind has devised to keep us from seeing wholeness. From our solar plexus, garbage and nutrients are merely different parts of the whole. The negative attitude toward garbage begins when we are babies in diapers. When the diapers need to be changed, we cry. If we are silent, no one changes them. Do you see the type of program set in motion with our early training?

If you have a mess in your life and you sit still, no one comes to help get rid of it, and you remain in the mess. If, on the other hand, you scream loudly enough, someone *will* come.

In our everyday world, no one can help get rid of the mess. The more you fight it, the longer you stay in it. Do you see what you are experiencing? How can we develop a trust in knowing that we will be able to move on from dwelling in garbage if we do not fight it ourselves? The banana fruit is pure, even though it is covered by what we later discard as garbage.

This is where faith comes in; not just simple letting-go (in your rational mind) but total surrendering, letting-go from the gut of your being.

A primary difficulty here is our wish to experience ''selective surrendering.'' We surrender only to that which is in the area of our *strength*. Rarely do we let go in an area where we are insecure. An analogy is the person who does not like to eat food, who preaches the virtue of fasting. True, it is good for the body to fast on occasion, but that person is not truly surrendering who fasts because he dislikes food.

Another example of ''selective surrendering'' is the metaphysical person who is strong intellectually. He/she can venture off into the realm of thoughts, feeling ''free'' to think whatever he/she wants, no matter what beliefs ''society'' holds to be true. The appearance of surrendering to the world of ideas seems open and liberally broadening, but because he/she has *already* such a mind, does not indicate liberation or true freedom. Where does he/she hold on to society's laws? Usually they hold on in the area of greatest vulnerability and fear, the area of least control, the area of feelings uncontrolled by the rational mind.

Love is one of the most sensitive areas where we need to totally surrender. To accomplish this, we need faith. Again, it is not faith that ''everything will work out'' in the relationship, but faith that you can only attract a person who will reflect where you are. This blessing in life is what is meant by having faith; not blind faith, but gut-level strength.

In his book of the same title, Dr. Jampolsky says, ''love is letting go of fear.'' However, knowing it is not enough. The Cosmic Warrior must digest and understand the dynamics of fear. Fear is being caught in your throat-and-neck-center, not knowing, trying to control because of fear and of not knowing. There is no room for love in fear. In love, we are free to let go, for worthiness and faith are not bascd on a person *outside of you*.

The mind, when it works through the throat-and-neck-center, is like a black hole in space, having the ability to deny anything, even light. It sees all that is beloved as apart from it, and becomes afraid of losing this love. The mind then seeks some means of control over the situation.

Who wants to let go of what is loved? Everyone wants to let go of what is not loved, and this is another example of "selective surrendering". Most people come to counseling in order to let go of something painful. Unless they are prepared to let go of joy, they will not be able to let go of pain.

The Cosmic Warrior knows it is not enough to let go, under only congenial conditions. But who will call a repair man when the washer is working?

It is like being alone without a love partner, without someone to share your embrace as well as thoughts and feelings. You want an intimate relationship more than anything else. Then, someone comes into your life and touches your heart. Are you ready to let that person go? The illusion is that the love the person appears to be sharing with you comes from outside of you. Understand the illusion of *love*, and you may let go and love forever. You will love forever, because *you* are the *love*.

Once the illusion is gone, you can share and never be

drained. You, by the law of this world, must attract another just like you. But, it is not enough to know in your mind that you *are* love; you must feel timelessness; you must never possess, nor be possessed. No holding back, no selfishness, no loss, no fear.

What is unique about this process is that it is not asking you to exchange old thoughts for new. It is saying, that wherever you are, you may make the step towards a remembrance of that which you are. What you believe, what you think (your ologies), are of no importance. Simply return to that which you have always been before you were told what you were, what you could be or should be.

I am not talking here about a "spaced-out" experience, but a movement to the center of this very moment. You do not have to go to India, nor wait until Christ returns. Did he ever leave? All it takes for that first step is to get out of your head and embrace and breathe through your gut. This is so important it must be experienced before you meditate, or else you will use meditation as a way to *get* something (i.e., higher consciousness, samadhi). If you think you do not already have "it," then trying to get "it" becomes the barrier. If you think you already have "it," then the thought of what you think "it" is, is itself limiting.

The first step to go out of your mind (throat-and-neck-center) is to breathe from your solar plexus, slowly, deeply, naturally. This is why the Way, the Tao, is one of time and timelessness. The Tao teaches us how to live in timelessness in the midst of a world of time and space. Jesus said in Matthew 18:3, ''. . . unless ye become as little children, ye shall not enter into the kingdom of heaven.'' Unless you breathe like a child from your solar plexus, you will not know you are in the kingdom *now*.

Only your mind has judged what spirituality, God and reality should be. I am saying when we cling to these concepts, we do so because we are afraid of not knowing and not having a reality system to cling to to be real.

During the first meditation I gave at my Temple, I asked all those present to ''throw God out'' of their lives. My parents were there, sitting proudly in the first row. Proud, that is, until I said to throw God out the door. The looks on their faces! What I was trying to say was to throw out the *concept* of God, a concept limited by the nature of the mind that holds it, so that the true God, Reality (infinite timelessness) may be embraced.

Are you willing to throw out God? The answer does not come from the mind. When you remember you are a Cosmic Warrior, you embrace the allness of life, without judgment. Even garbage is embraced. There is no pain, no sin, no evil.

CHAPTER 4

Breathe Free, Be Free

DURING THE NINE MONTHS in our mother's womb, our source of nourishment comes from the umbilical cord connected at our solar plexus. We are fed, therefore, not at the mouth, but at the gut. In yoga, this center is called the Manipura Chakra (the Marsian chakra or wheel), the wheel of desire.

Through desire we are drawn into this world. We did not come into it pretending we were not supposed to be here; yet by understanding the wheel and embracing desire, we are free. Fight this same desire, and it will control us. Out of fear there is always the urge to control that which appears to be outside.

After nine months, we enter this world and take our first breath. Our addiction to breathing has begun. Naturally, this is the last desire we let go.

Buddha is always pictured as having a rather large

belly, but he was not fat. Symbolically, Buddha's belly shows he was centered in his solar plexus. It is from this belly that we are fed. Locked up in the throat-and-neck-center, we may eat and never be full. In the mind, we are never truly filled; needing more, we continue to eat.

Knowledge, by itself, feeds only the mind, leaving us feeling empty. It is through *digestion* that *knowledge* becomes wisdom and fills the self so that there is no more hunger. Being fulfilled, however, is not like stuffing our body with a Thanksgiving dinner. We do not become lethargic. It is not a peacefulness that puts us to sleep. When we are fulfilled we are fearless, no longer held back by self doubt. We feel a strength that does not push us to control and conquer. The mind is like rowing a boat with one oar. Use one oar by itself and we will continually go around in circles. The other oar is our solar plexus—where our feelings and intuition live. By breathing from your solar plexus you use both oars. The key to knowing our path is time. When we are connected to our path there is no time.

This movement into the solar plexus center is not a movement *away* from the world, but a movement into the center of whatever is happening. Breathing from this center will initiate the birth of the Cosmic Warrior.

If you insist on staying up in your throat-and-neck center, it will all become like an eternal Pac Man game. This game reflects the continual frustration plaguing mankind and has therefore become one of the most popular video games. If you have never seen or played the game, go out and do so and you will know what I mean. You are the Pac Man and you run around the board trying to eat up (accumulate) as many dots (points, dollars) as you can. But look out, the four ghosts begin to chase you and try to eat you up. One of them, by the way, just happens to be named, "Shadow." After eating up as many dots as you can in one area, you eat a power pill (achievement, promotion). The power pill gives you the ability to chase and eat up the ghosts. But the power does not last very long and different strategies lead you off into new directions, more dots, more power pills and occasional cherry rewards, but it is never enough. After you clear the board of all the dots and power pills is the game over? No, you are given a brand new game board with more dots, power pills, and hungry ghosts trying to devour you. The only way the game ends is when you get eaten up (deflated) a number of times. If you avoid the ghost, you can never rest. Either way, you get eaten up. Winning takes the form of comparing your score with that of another who is also playing the game. You both get eaten up, but one of you has acquired more points. The game uses you.

The question is: can we let go and still play the game? The answer is that it is the *only* way we can play! The Cosmic Warrior's path is not avoidance, but rather a path of direct confrontation with whatever *is*. Those who have always tried to *appear* to be strong (in their image of what strength is) have, in reality, been the most fearful. We live in a society which substantiates that the more money you have, the better you are as a person. The result of such thinking is insecure people pushing to make money to hide behind. It is not *what* you do, it is the *reason* you do it that is important. Are you living to serve an image you have been trying to create, or are you living true to your being? The birth of the Cosmic Warrior is the birth into honesty, an openness that is the greatest of all strengths.

> To thine own self be true, for as night time shall follow the day, thou canst not be false to any man.
>
> —Shakespeare

From babyhood we face the fear of whether we will be loved for, not only our bright side, but for our dark side as well. To handle wholeness, the Cosmic Warrior learns to embrace the dark side, the part of our inner nature we fear the most. To repress our dark side is to close off wholeness, and be forced to live an image, a role that will surely suffocate us. The key to our healthiness is not through fighting our dark side (either in ourselves or as projected on others) but embracing it and, in doing so, embracing our wholeness.

Many books have been written about the dark side, the shadow, the guardian of the gate. I am not going into all that others have said, but I must reiterate that the first step to embrace your wholeness is to breathe naturally, slowly, deeply from your solar plexus. It is when you choke up in the throat that you lose control. We are told to take a deep breath and count to ten. Get out of your head, your emotional center, and into your gut, your feeling center. Feelings run deep; emotions change continually. In the midst of all the whirl and swirl, you are at rest—still in the midst of it all, but you do not grab on, you do not take this image or that image. You are not this thought or that thought. You are. That is all. The mind demands feedback on images and thoughts.

In a float tank (isolation tank designed by John Lilly for inner exploration beyond the senses) with the absence of sound, touch and sight, new images are still created by the mind. The need to have *something* as *manifest reality* takes over. The fear of the mind is that if it lets go, one will live in utter emptiness, a void.

> We shall not cease from exploration
> And the end of all our exploring
> Will be to arrive where we started
> And know the place for the first time.
> —T.S. Eliot
> from *Four Quartets*

When true letting go takes place, you live in timelessness in the midst of earth existence:

The Zen Master asked by a disciple to describe how his life had changed after he experienced his enlightenment:

''Before I was enlightened when I got up in the morning, I would wash, have breakfast and chop wood. Now when I get up, I wash, have breakfast and chop wood.''

—An old teaching story

CHAPTER 5

Embracing the Dark Side

Once upon a time, male-female relationships were more easily defined: a man was a "man" and a woman was a "woman." On a first date, you did "this," and on a second date you did "that." However, as America entered the 1960's, many people were not satisfied with the old definitions. They wanted freedom to relate what they *could* be, not what they *had* to be.

Today, no one knows who is supposed to pick up the tab on a first date, or whether it should be shared. I am not going to talk about women's liberation, but about people's liberation. Think about how "locked-in" men were when they insisted on keeping women "locked-in." Our behavior was geared primarily to outer appearances. The Cosmic Warrior learns to look within.

It is only with the heart that one can see clearly, what is essential is "invisible" to the eyes.
— The Fox to the Little Prince

Today, we no longer accept the sexual role as it is seen from the outside. Now, we have to go within to confront the unknown. If we are lying to ourselves, we will not be sure of the other person's honesty.

Questions: how can we tell if someone is honest . . . how can we trust . . . how can we know that which cannot be seen externally?

Do you know the game the extrovert plays with the introvert?

The extrovert: "Come on, tell me what you are thinking. I'll tell you what I am thinking."

Quiet.

The extrovert: "If you were thinking nice thoughts, you would want to tell me. But, because you are not talking, you must be thinking unpleasant thoughts."

Without the introvert saying a word, the extrovert thinks he knows what the other is thinking by pure projection (of his own nature). As we become more understanding of who we are, we are free from having to live according to surface images. We also become more aware that the "old" surface images and roles cannot simply be replaced by "New Age" role images. In Tibetan Buddhism, the concept would be described as having moved on from our chains of *iron* (old archaic images and concepts of reality) to chains of *gold* (New Age consciousness).

But, whether iron or gold, they are still chains. The image of spirituality has taken on a new appearance. To be enlightened means __________ (you fill in the blank).

I believe we must throw our answer away, and just be. Now, throw that away and breathe from the solar plexus. But images still crowd the mind with fears of what happens after we let go. These fears will always live up in the throat-and-neck center.

Maybe the answer is that everything is "all right" as it is. I am not talking about what is *seen* from the chaos of the rational mind, but what is *felt* from the gut center, which is a manifestation of balance, order and justice. Isn't this issue of justice one of the major themes the rational mind has struggled with throughout the centuries? Maybe trying to make it the "right way" upsets our natural balance. I do not mean a neutral balance where nothing is moving or alive, but a dynamic yin-yang, warp-woof, in-out balance, where the universe is filled with spontaneity and change; a balance where you do not have to do anything but be. While focusing predominantly on the male nature in our culture, with its rationality and logic, the female nature with its intuition and feeling is under-valued.

Instead of seeing illness as "wrong" and trying to remove it, we ought to see it as an inner message speaking directly to the patient. Accidents and difficulties in relationships are perfect reflections of what is happening within. Only the ego (throat-and-neck center) sees them as separate.

In a fairytale, the dark side is like a trouble-maker (an uninvited guest) whom you don't invite to your party. You did not send an invitation, but the troublemaker finds out and decides to come to your party anyway. What is the dark, shadowy element that keeps you from feeling whole? Is it sex, anger, control, fear? What is it in *your* world that sets you off so intensely that you have to make up laws to protect you from it?

In order to prevent the unexpected appearance of our dark side, these laws we set up appear to be the blockages and are treated as if they were the problem. The real issue is what made us create the laws in the first place? To knock down someone's walls, and tear apart his laws in an effort to help save him, shows no understanding or compassion for that person. The walls are not the issue. That type of experience will just encourage the person next time to build stronger walls and make tougher laws with the issue firmly rooted and intact. The person must want to move on, and just his saying ''help'' does not always mean he is ready. You cannot save people or help them. This implies that they have a problem and that something is wrong and all you will end up doing is studying wall ''ology.'' Nothing is wrong. Their situation is a perfect reflection of what they are doing. Do not try to take it away to help them.

When we are ready to change—to give up our laws, to be unafraid of the dark side—we have had quite literally, all the pain we can take. Painful situations are our teachers. If we try to pull away from pain (illness, relationships, accidents) before the right moment, we will run back and hold on more deliberately than before.

Because you do not run after them to save them, some people will think you don't care. You have to give people room to have their pain. How many parents have tried to ''save'' their child from marrying the wrong person only to end up pushing him or her into the marriage by doing sò?

I am now addressing the doctor, therapist, counselor, healer, minister, spiritual teacher. This is *your* dark side. The fear of having others, as well as yourselves, see you as *unable* to take away someone's pain, or worse, their thinking you do not *care*. You must distinguish between a cut artery that you must put pressure on to stop the bleeding and emotional ranting and ravings that must be given their room. There is no need to cure or save; everything is in order. When this moment is embraced, you may move on, but until that time you will forever be fighting your inner fear, your shadow. By fighting it, you feed it. Remember, throughout our everyday lives, we are all teachers, counselors, and therapists for one another.

By embracing the shadow—the dark side of your nature—you do not become a masochist, you realize your freedom. If you make a change by thinking something outside of you is locking you in, you move into yet another similar trap. (Chains of iron, chains of gold.) The trap was not the old way of looking at the world or the old way of thinking. Nor will the new way lead us to liberation. We are already liberated.

When any new therapy hits the market, it temporarily changes our focus from the old pattern of pain to a new pattern. We feel a great sense of relief. Given time, however, the new pattern becomes as painful as the old. The therapist (the-rapist) simply helps shift the pattern from a wornout, painful one, to a new one filled with hopes and promises that things will be better. Nothing outside you can help. That is the grand illusion.

Now you must embrace the true healer, you, the one who is already healed, the Christ within; embrace timelessness in a world of time and space.

CHAPTER 6

Sex and Relationships

THE FEELING OF MOVING into orgasm, which takes place not just when you have sexual intercourse or masturbate, but every moment, is at its height a feeling of timelessness that quite literally lifts you out of your head. We crave this feeling of release, but unfortunately, have only associated it with sexuality.

When we believe that it is only with the *right* partner or image that we may reach orgasm, we attempt to possess that person and become possessed and controlled by him or her. Sexual orgasm is as close as most people actually get to living in timelessness consciously. There are so many fears surrounding our sexuality that this theme is a prime mover in today's subliminal commercial advertising market. The problem is that sex is a purely gut-centered experience, which, for most people, remains in the head.

In essence, if you breathe slowly and deeply from your gut, you will extend orgasm by experiencing timelessness. Staying in your head, you block out true sexuality, and therefore, can only be involved with people who are doing the same thing. Locking up in the throat-and-neck area may prevent you from enjoying sex or from experiencing orgasm. Remember, it is the ideas and images of who you are that get in the way and add to the blockage. The church in our Western culture, realizing the power of orgasm, made a judgement against sex by confusing it with guilt to keep us locked in our heads.

In addition to that, some of us were asked to bow our heads to pray. When you bow your head, you put a kink in the spinal column hose. Your inner current which runs up and down your spinal column gets blocked up in the land of beliefs, locking you into your thoughts and images. I am not saying do not pray; just keep your spine straight when you do.

Another blockage that relates to the same area is thinking that you are either a male or a female. Your limited attitudes toward sexuality will inhibit your response and sharing. Traditionally, men have been afraid to receive (to be receptive) and women have been told not to be aggressive (to be feminine). Control was the real issue here, and it prohibited a sharing, loving, sexual relationship. I am not trying to tell you what a ''correct'' relationship ought to be. However, the minute you get out of your head and into your gut, you will know what you need.

If you are in a prison (in your head) and think about all the things you will do when you get out of prison (move to your gut center), those things will seem wild and reckless compared to what you will do when you are actually free. Being in prison distorts your perception. If you are free in your gut, your actions will not be chaotic for you. But, if you are caught up in your throat-and-neck center, everything you do will be a chaotic attempt at getting free, or worse, showing everyone how *free* you are. People who run around trying to push their freedom on others do not feel as free inside as they would like others to think.

The real question is, how do we maintain that feeling of orgasm at every moment when we are with someone we love? The feeling is timeless. Time passing so quickly, it dissolves. To make love with one you love is natural because the tingle and timelessness that you feel when you fall in love are the same that you feel when you have an orgasm. And to share that is true ecstasy. But what happens is you do not want to lose that feeling, and the minute you try to possess it, ''it'' is gone. That explains why some of the most beautiful and painful times are shared with the same person. We do not consciously plan it that way—here I am reminded of a line used by comedian Steve Martin,

You really have to know someone and love them before you can abuse and degrade them.

You can't just run up to a stranger on the street and yell and scream at him; you have to get to know him first. After you say you love him and feel somewhat secure in the relationship, you open your door and release your pain. When this happens, you lose the feeling of timelessness in the relationship because you have already *judged* what a loving relationship should be.

The battle and pain are within, and we draw in partnerships to show us this, as in the case of people who remarry the ''same type of person.'' We need the tingle to remain alive in our relationship. The only way to ensure it is to make a commitment to living in the *now*, one moment at a time.

Relating is a key. Sharing is a key. Communicating is a key. But unless timelessness occurs, there is no spark, no tingle to keep the door of sharing open. That spark, that tingle, is being alive in the midst of the bright side as well as the dark side. The head cannot create timelessness; only an illusion tells us we can.

We must free ourselves of the images of what we *think* love is; they get in the way. The image of being a man, being a woman stands in the way of the sharing. You can *know* in your mind love is the answer, but can you *feel* it? Breathe in, stomach out, slowly and deeply. Breathe out, the stomach goes in.

Relationships teach you to face the seasons of this life's experience, to have an opportunity to open the door to the most intimate "you." This sharing is not a clinging to the other person, but rather a letting-go-and-living. And it is not a letting go out of *not caring*, but a letting go *because* of caring. Further, it is not just *thinking* you know this, but *feeling* and living it each and every moment.

The point is not being afraid to let go and face what is. Fear holds us back, but let's not get caught in the "analysis paralysis" of playing the game of "let's figure out the fear." This indicates there is a problem to be solved. There is no problem; everything is all right as it is. Move on, breathe into and embrace what you have been fighting. The mind will try to reason you out of such a simple decision, but in your heart, remember the promises the mind has made, the answers it has given, and yet your hunger continues. The mind wants control.

Do not destroy the mind; just embrace your gut and live in the midst of your orgasm. When you connect with that wonderment, you see sex as yet another moment through which orgasm is shared.

Creativity is a channel through which the master expresses being. The masterpiece is timeless. The Cosmic Warrior is born in this moment of meditation when the lover and beloved have become one through the act of loving.

CHAPTER 7

Addiction: Drugs and the Drugged

We ARE ALL ADDICTED to something. Naturally, what we become addicted to controls us, and when we are controlled, we lose our freedom and forget who we are. Life becomes cloudy.

How will you release your last breath? With a gasp and struggle to get one more, or with a sigh, letting go?

How are you breathing now? Do you know that when you smoke, you alter your breathing pattern? It is not the cigarette tobacco that relaxes you, it is the deep inhalation and exhalation response, a slowing of the body-mind's rhythm.

Do you remember how you struggled to regain breath after a trauma—such as a near drowning or choking? From the moment you were born and took your first breath, you were addicted; one more breath, your mind keeps chanting, over and over. As much as you love to

47

breathe, you have to let go of breath as well. Do not worry, it will come back, but you must let it go.

If you know how to die, you know how to live. You are neither the inbreath nor the outbreath, coolness nor warmth. You are that which is in between the two breaths. By simply observing your breath, a great mystery is revealed. As you can see, throughout the book, the main theme is that breathing is something we all, right at this moment, have in common. It is the doorway to forgetfulness as well as the golden key to remembering. The illusion the mind tells us is that we think we already know. I am a man, I am a woman, I am black, I am white, I am an American, I am Chinese and so on, the mind goes on and on. But, do we need all those I.D.'s? The more we don't know, the more uncertain we are of our true nature, the more we cling to identification images, and will go to great extremes to defend them.

It makes for a good movie, doesn't it? Yet, when you embrace the wholeness, all these individual parts still remain, part of the whole, not apart from it. Our life is like a movie we like so much that we are driven to see it over and over again, even though we already know the ending. It is the theme, the inner meaning that touches us. It is like a ski run that we know by heart. We also know exactly where it will end. Yet, we still like to ski down it because of the feeling we get when we let go as we go down the hill.

An addiction is that which separates us from the awareness of our wholeness. An example is using your rational mind as your sole focus on reality. This addiction will drive you crazy trying to understand the infinite with the perspective of the finite mind.

Another form of addiction feeds off this first example. In an attempt to keep the finite mind intact while it tries to understand the infinite, a person becomes addicted to one thought or belief in order to dull the mind. Often such a condition of desperation manifests as a fundamentalist doctrine in religion which says, have faith, just believe, do not ask questions.

People who are strongly against "chemical drugs," are often caught up in "thought drugs," and consequently, must get rid of all "drug addicts" who remind them of their own inner addiction. The "700 Club" (a Christian evangelistic T.V. program) discusses, on a daily basis, chemical drug abuse in our society. But, who is addicted? I am saying the issue is clearly not drugs: it is addiction.

What are we addicted to? One thing I do not like about marijuana is that users associate their "high" feeling with the drug. They say the drug "does it" for them. Everyone always wants to find a rationale for why they feel high; perhaps so they can use something else as a rationale for why they are not feeling high. Excuses, hooks, you name it, people use them. Blame parents, wife, kids, friends. At the base of every addiction is the opportunity to point at the *outside* and say, "there is the culprit." It is always something *outside* which is responsible.

One of the most difficult times in our personal growth is when everything is going well around us, and yet we feel depressed. The rational mind enjoys attacking self-worth with all kinds of unfounded but perfectly supportable non-reasonings. The answer to this dilemma is in not taking responsibility for your life in the head, but in the gut. With responsibility in the head, control and power become necessary to ego-survival.

Our biggest addiction, next to our breath, is that we think that our life is outside of us and we are separate from it. That is what the eyes report, and until we have seen enough professional stage magic to know how easily the eyes are fooled, we still probably believe that the woman is sawed in half!

We are addicted to the illusion, and we crave it like we crave the magic show. When we learn how to do a few magic tricks, it is hard to believe that we were ever fooled by them because they are so simple. Of course, life itself is the grand illusion, but even when you know the nature of the illusion, you still love to share it with others.

If you were going to live in eternity, what would you do? Doing is constant strain, being is timeless, pure consciousness. We have become creatures of habit and that habit is one of unconsciousness. To break the addiction of unconsciousness, breathe deeply and circulate your current, participate in what you love to do from the very core of your being.

The question may be—what moves you? Can you love that which moves you so much that you won't fear becoming addicted to it? Can you love it so much that you are also willing to let it go? What made you think you had it in the first place?

The thought of holding on and possessing that which you love means you are taking the future for granted, forgetting to live in the only true moment, NOW.

The Cosmic Warrior is not addicted, so he does not become a drug for others. Others needing a drug will think he does not care. The world has many drugs. Be aware that freedom, knowledge, even higher consciousness, can be addicting. Freedom from addiction is the movement from the throat-and-neck-center to the solar plexus.

CHAPTER 8

Laughter

How many times have you heard "laughter is the best medicine?" It is true. When you laugh, a deep gut-busting laugh, you leave your head and there is a release of tension from the throat center.

"I almost died laughing." A strange but accurate statement for when you truly laugh, you do die, your ego does, anyway. When you are afraid, you tighten up at the neck and breathe more rapidly. People who are "up tight," in the throat center that is, have a difficult time laughing.

One of my teachers always said there is a difference between *seriousness* and *sincerity*. Many times a person laughing is not seen as sincere. To laugh at yourself is a great gift, and it does not have to mean you are insincere. It is that people get so serious in their attempt to appear sincere (a cover for fear) they forget *how* to laugh.

I enjoy watching stand-up comedy at a local comedy club. Some of the funniest moments on stage take place when the performer drops his routine and shares spontaneously with the audience. The funniest comedians have the ability to make their routine appear to happen spontaneously, as if each moment is the first run. That is quite a feat because most comedians have worked a routine hundreds of times. If the routine does not control them, they can let go and enjoy the moment along with the audience. This becomes a sharing of laughter between audience and comedian. However, the ego's fear of failure prevents such sharing and the comedian, no matter how professional, seems stiff, unyielding.

One of the key ingredients in laughter is being caught ''off guard.'' If you expect something, such as a logical answer, and you get the opposite, the result will be funny. Fear—in this example—though, will produce a form of laughter which is a defense protecting us from our fear. It becomes the shallow, staccato laughter you hear in an audience watching a horror movie. On the screen the most gruesome effects are taking place in living color, and yet the audience is laughing. Not a deep gut level laughter, but a nervous laughter, from the throat center, out of fear.

When I apply laughter to my daily work, I tell stories.

A lady comes into my office for consultation. One of the first issues she wants to go into is her tennis serve. When she is playing tennis she chokes up every time she begins to serve. I tell her that I can immediately cut her problem in half. Her eyes light up and she asks me, ''How?'' I say, ''Next time, play doubles!''

One of my favorite stories was told by Woody Allen at the beginning of his movie ''Annie Hall.''

Two elderly women are at a Catskill Mountain resort and one of them says, ''Boy, the food at this place is really terrible.'' ''Yes, I know'', says the other one—''and such small portions.'' ''Well that's how I feel about life: full of loneliness, misery, suffering and unhappiness, and it's over much too quickly.''

The point is that we all need laughter in our lives, laughter being a form of therapy, which like diaphragmatic breathing, takes us out of the constrictions of the throat-and-neck-center.

I am not saying that you will never cry—we will always have our seasons in nature—but in the midst of it all, there is laughter. The closer you move to the center of your being, your anger dissolves, you feel warmth, and the nearness of laughter. Again, it is a timeless experience.

Is your God laughing or is He angry?

CHAPTER 9

Death

UNLESS YOU CAN DIE, you cannot be truly alive. The rational mind does not live comfortably in the midst of the infinite with its need for definite beginnings and endings. The linear programming of the rational mind craves knowing, and this need is reflected in all the writings concerning death, afterlife and reincarnation.

By awakening the Cosmic Warrior within, one lives in the center of what is called the wheel of life and death. The purpose of this chapter is not to tell you to believe in heaven or hell, or even to encourage you to believe in reincarnation. What you must discover is what *you know to be true* on your own. Other than through direct experience, all the rest is a belief system, or purely intellectual philosophy. Belief is not enough; you must have direct experience. To *talk* about the nature of death, or to *deny* that this is a part of *life* needing open exploration, is to ignore the essential cycle of life.

The movement into direct experience is the life path of the Cosmic Warrior. However, direct experience alone is still not enough; you must digest the experience. There is a lot of eating going on, yet still people hunger. The underlying question here is, do you believe you have the right to that direct experience? My saying that it is your birthright is not enough; you must *know* you have the right. You must throw out all that you have been taught about death, afterlife, reincarnation to understand the experience. For all you know, when your body goes to sleep at night, you die. In some Hindu cultures, sleep is called the "little death." What is your ritual before you leave this physical plane every evening as you prepare for sleep?

Death implies an ending. From the throat-and-neck center, death of the physical body *is* an ending. The ego dies. However, when you are in your solar plexus, you embrace the constant sea of change and transformation, instead of the parade of opposites and fears in your mind.

To be told by the metaphysician that there is no death and that life is eternal, is fine. But are you *living* your eternity now? "I know," says the mind, "that I am not the body," but when the Zen Master hits you on the head with his stick, you say, "Ouch, why did you hurt me?"

Are you truly knowing? To be alive, you must embrace death as well as what you have been calling life: life and death dance hand in hand. They are just another dance of opposites in the land of reflection.

Today, the Hospice movement is growing in America. Those working in this program are sharing openly and honestly with both the individuals and their families who are in the midst of the dying experience. They share the here and now, the precious moment, the sense of acceptance, not taking any other moment for granted.

We are born into this world with a terminal illness, though most of us do not know when our bodies will die. Some find out that they have cancer, for example, and are told they have six months to live. Suddenly they seem to stop taking their life for granted. Have you been doing this with your life?

If you do not live in eternity, now, what makes you think you will do so after your body dies? We get lost in dreams, yet dreams (desires) are the direct path back to the dreamer. With each cycle of breath (in breath—out breath) there is birth, sustenance, death.

It is so simple to observe the breath. But because it is so simple to do, the mind will find many ways to block this natural technique for remembering timelessness. What is so beautiful is that after you remember, you can return to ''ologies'' and ''osophies.'' But now your heart will be along with you.

There is nothing wrong with any path you choose. They are all vehicles, but you need to feed them because they are essentially lifeless. They cannot feed you; you must bring life to them. To live in the ''now'' is to live in timelessness, where there is no birth or death: void of existence, but a state of awareness through which you bring life to all that you touch.

CHAPTER 10

Meditation

IF YOU ARE MEDITATING to ''get something,'' you are not meditating. Meditation does not teach the science of ''getology.'' The rational mind believes, unless you get something from what you are doing, there is no reason to do it.

Haven't you lost something and spent a frantic hour searching for it? After you have reached your limit, exhausted from looking everywhere, you sit back at a total loss for where the item could be. Out of nowhere, its whereabouts pops into your head. Without doing anything, the item you've been frantically searching for appears.

Remembering, you become conscious of the moment. Forgetting, you are unconscious. Of your life's experiences, see which memories stand out in your mind.

The ones which come back were moments of consciousness. Look how much we forget. The unique experience about the remembered moments is that they are timeless. They may have occurred years ago, yet you remember them as if they happened today. We need to *remember* our connection in timelessness.

The techniques of meditation are designed to help you remember what is ever and always there. This remembrance creates a paradox with our time and space world. You find yourself falling in love, feeling as if the person you have recently met is someone you have known for years. Yet, after actually knowing him for years, each day seems fresh, as though you had just met.

Meditation allows you to see the newness, the nowness in everyday relationships. You cannot truly experience meditation until your breath is free of your throat center, and you embrace your solar plexus. That freeing of breath gives the mind room to think thoughts freely and not struggle with them. What else is a mind to do? You fight it and you feed it.

Meditation is not to be confused with a *technique*. Techniques do not give illumination, which is already there. Meditation is the *digested experience*. Techniques that promise *something* cannot reveal the *no-thing*. The mind can also sit back, get spiritually lazy and say, "Since I already have it, I do not need to meditate, do Hatha Yoga, fast, go to a workshop. I might as well do something I really love to do.'' I say, do it, do what you love, do it one hundred percent. Take whatever you love doing and totally embrace it. You will feel the tingle and circulation of your current. That is a path of devotion. You will see ''you'' in the midst of your path. I do not mean do something because you were or were not told to do it. Do it because you *feel* it. You need to know you know without the belief or wish that it is true. I am not talking about knowing the nature of the dream; I am talking about knowing the dreamer.

Meditation is not an excuse to pull away from the world, but an opportunity to move deeper into it. While living in a world of doing, reasoning and questioning, to sit down, do ''nothing,'' is a gift. It puts life in perspective without telling you what the perspective is or should be. Do not worry about choosing a Guru, therapist, teacher, or technique; you will draw-in the one who most completely reflects your need. There are no false teachers, just perfect mirrors.

As he bent over for a drink, the crest jewel accidentally dropped into the lake from the Maharaj's turban. He ordered hundreds of his servants into the lake to find it. For many hours the servants thrashed around looking for the jewel, always coming up empty-handed. A little yogi (wise man) stepped forward and told the Maharaj he could find it. But, only if he could have total control over the recovery operation. This request was granted. The yogi then ordered all the servants out of the lake and he then proceeded to sit on the shore not doing a thing. The Maharaj protested, saying how could he possibly find the jewel while sitting on the shore and not attempting to look for it in the water. The yogi reminded him of his promise and continued to sit. As he sat, the muddy waters of the lake settled. After an hour, he got up and looked into the clear, calm lake, and saw a lump on the bottom and bent over and picked up the crest jewel.

—An old teaching story

We live on an earth that is spinning on its axis as it revolves around a star. These movements create our time references of days and years. We get dizzy and lost in time on earth. The dizziness is a form of hypnosis that makes us believe we are earthlings living in time. Meditation takes us into the center of our mind-body complex where there is no spinning, no dizziness, no hypnotic spell, no time. The mathematical point at the center of a spinning wheel is at rest; it does not spin, like the eye of a hurricane. Meditation reminds us of that which is, not what we think should be. We live in the ''peace'' of the center, not lost in the swirl. We meditate to remember this, for how can we get something that we already have?

Prayer and affirmations are used to "get something." Meditation is the digested experience that reminds you that you already live in the midst of timelessness. But first, before you meditate, breathe naturally from your solar plexus, allow the muddy water of your mind to settle.

CHAPTER 11

Religion

T HE KEY TO THE beginning of most religions has been a
direct experience by one individual. From that one individual's direct experience, the followers are fed, by
belief. We are moving from an ''Age of Belief'' that has
been with us for 2,000 years and are now preparing to
move into an ''Age of Knowing.'' Buddha said it thus—
''No one can eat for you, no one can sleep for you, no
one can drink for you; what makes you think someone
can be illuminated for you? You must seek your own illumination with great diligence.''

Does your religion *ask* you to believe, or does it guide
you into your own direct experience? Religion should be
the guide to teach you how to move into experience en-
tirely on your own.

> If you give a man a fish he will eat for one day.
> If you teach him to fish, he will eat forever.
>
> —Old teaching proverb

Religion is not the recitation of scripture; such a practice keeps the "experience" up in the head. The Cosmic Warrior is the fountainhead of the waters of the "New Age" of knowing, filling the thirst of those still clinging to belief. Teaching others how to fish, his message is that each of us has the right to direct experience. Religion should be the vehicle showing us how to avoid the limitations of the mind, enabling us to embrace Allness. The true surrendering is not *to* God but *with* God.

Is your religion based on your being sick or healthy? Does it remove sin or celebrate your wholeness (holiness)? The so-called "sick religion" will have to change when more people begin to love themselves.

Only two commandments were said to be given by Jesus, the Christ:

"You must love the Lord your God with all your heart, and with all your soul, and with all your strength, and with all your mind. And you must love your neighbor just as much as you love yourself." Luke 10:27.

Does your religion proclaim to be a religion of love, which, nonetheless, is alienated from all who do not accept its tenets?

Are you worthy? Happy?

What *do* you believe?

Questions, questions, overloading the rational mind. The teachers of fundamental religious truth say one way to salvation is to believe; then you will be saved. With so many books about truth available today, how do you know who is speaking truth? Is the devil that which makes you doubt, fight against yourself?

The devil, diablos, is the divided one, another symbol of your mind, your church. The devil separates everything into good and bad, and at a moment's whim, turns that around. Do not fight the devil; you will feed him if you do. Embrace your solar plexus and see how the devil is a part of the kingdom of God.

This experience from your solar plexus is the key to experiencing, not the God of Light, nor worshipping the God of Darkness, but that which is at the center, making experience possible. Religion is the vehicle to embrace the experience *within*. In the past, you had an inner experience and responded to your religious calling. Now you go to religion *for* the experience. I am talking of *having, receiving* and *remembering* your religious experience in the midst of your everyday life. You do not have to go to a monastery or make a pilgrimage to India. You will still get up each morning, have breakfast, chop wood. Your religious beliefs or disbeliefs form the basis of your life, and religion has been the way, historically, that you could have contact with the unknown.

But we have mistaken the institution and its beliefs that we have made contact with, for the unknown. This is like the finger pointing toward the moon being mistaken for the moon.

All religious pathways are vehicles, not the answers. You are the answer.

When I entered the seminary in a Hindu Temple, my teacher told me that I must follow only one dogma, and that was to seek "truth." Remember how afraid the Catholic Church was when the great astronomers Galileo and Copernicus wanted to declare that the sun, not the earth, was at the center of our solar system? We are at that same turning point today.

Who is at the center?

CHAPTER 12

Astrology

THE ASTROLOGY I WANT to discuss is not found in the horoscope column of your daily newspaper. I want to go beyond the popular image of astrology into the essence of this empirical (observable) science. When I look at the horoscope of an individual, the doorway of his Soul, his memory track, the collective unconscious, opens before me. The chart is like a mandala which opens the doors of my perception. I use this tool of Astrology to make immediate and direct contact with my client, allowing me to enter *with* him, without separation, into the midst of his life experience. The time involved in making contact with a person dissolves as we arrive at the doorstep of the issue he/she is focusing upon.

The people who come into my office are ready to share

a timeless experience. An hour appointment seems to be over in ten minutes. The individual knows that, when he/she comes in for a counselling session, I am not going to recite Linda Goodman's *Sun Sign* book, or talk about whether his/her daughter will marry next year. We get in touch with the individual's true nature, seasons, life cycles. There is no judgment of right or wrong, but an understanding of beginning where we are right now. By looking at an individual's chart, I can see where he/she is on the "inside." The image (persona) projected into the world is but a mask seeking acceptance. During a reading I go beyond this image into the gut, embracing the total person who lives inside/out. The chart reading is not designed to lock a person into time and space by defining his/her nature. I do not sit there talking of untapped potential. Together, we discuss the blockages to fulfillment.

However, knowing and describing blockages is not enough. The first step is to get the breathing out of the throat-and-neck center and into the gut so that the mind is relieved of trying to handle all the changes in a person's life. The fresh perspective this breathing offers the mind is like the plowing of a field before the new seeds are planted. Unless the mind is quieted, we cannot see what is in front of us. When the mind is restless, we become like a drowning person who has forgotten to swim.

The horoscope shows how the inner nature of our being attracts another, who, on the outside, appears totally different but on the inside is exactly the same as we are. The law in this universe is "like attracts like." To understand the timing of seasons in nature is to know the best time to do something. During the winter months, it is not *wrong* to plant; it is simply *not time*. There is a difference between the judgment of right and wrong, and knowing the nature of our seasons.

> And God said, let there be lights in the firmament of the heaven to divide the day from the night, and let them be for *signs* and for seasons and for days and years.
>
> —Bible, *Genesis* 1:14

> To everything there is a season, and a time to every purpose under the heaven.
>
> —Bible, *Ecclesiastes* 3:1

The horoscope shows the changing seasons internal. When you attune to them, you are free. When you know the law, it automatically sets you free. When you do not know the seasons and fight with them, you are trapped. When you breathe from your throat-and-neck center, you are trapped in your head.

People come to a reading during a time of change.

Rather than put the change in order, we find how change *is* the order. Whatever is happening around us is a perfect reflection for what we see within. In other words, reality ''works'' when we are living our lives honestly from the gut of our being; whereas, locked in our minds, we experience all kinds of injustice.

The horoscope shows the many ways people view reality. When you begin to understand the nature of the chart, you learn different viewpoints, and give others room for their unique life experience and understanding. This is another way of saying you will not get mad at a Frenchman if he does not speak Spanish. You learn to give people room to be who they are. You do not get mad at an Aries if he does not act like a Capricorn. You allow people the freedom to attend the movie of their own choice.

The best time to have your chart read is when you are a baby. Then your parents can see your nature as you are and not as they think a baby should be. The idea is to open up the limiting idea people have of their children, to see each child with his/her unique needs, without the interference of parental projection.

Teachers can use this as a tool for understanding their students. Dr. Ira Progoff, founder of the Dialogue House Workshop in New York City, told me that before he did doctoral work with Dr. Carl Jung, Jung had their horoscopes compared for compatability.

The horoscope wheel is a picture of the inner desires with which you were born. It is a map of our Soul. The planets in the heavens at the moment you were born, reflect the patterns within your Soul. "As above, so below." The planets do not cause events to happen or mold personalities. The planets are inner symbols (archetypes) that reflect what is happening. There is nothing to blame outside of you for what is happening in your life. Saturn and Mars are not at fault. These symbols in the horoscope reveal the parts of you that you are "understanding" or "not understanding."

When clients come in for a reading, I want to show that every situation in life is *showing* them a part of *themselves*. This is a big personal step because it represents a movement toward taking full responsibility for their own life. By fighting a part of the self we do not like, we feed it energy and draw a situation into our life that reflects this struggle.

The horoscope, like any system, is a tool. How we use the tool is up to us. The Cosmic Warrior sees this tool as a step toward a "New Age" psychology of understanding the movement toward remembering who we are in the midst of time and space.

My logo ⊖⊕ symbolizes the coming together of male (♂ Mars) and female (♀ Venus). This union brings forth a sense of expansion (♐ Sagittarius) in the midst of infinity ∞. Yet in this union, the male and female do not neutralize each other; they remain intact. This logo came to me during a meditation in 1971 and touched me deeply. The word ''symbol'' is derived from the word ''symbolos,'' which means to unify. I use the tool of Astrology in my counselling service to gain insight about the path we walk towards remembering our union. The impact of a symbol takes us to a place where words cannot go.

CHAPTER 13

The New Age

THERE HAS BEEN A considerable amount of talk about moving into a "New Age." Fritjof Capra's book, *The Turning Point*, is an excellent text for a beginning understanding of the transformations that are taking place throughout our culture. We are experiencing the end of the "Age of Belief" (Picean Age) where everyone believed without question. Now we are moving into the "Age of Knowing" (Aquarian Age) where we all demand our right to know. The question is whether we want to know only that which we believe to be true. Or do we want the whole truth, the holy truth? Do we want to know *everything* that goes on? Are we ready for our images of the world and of our parents to be shattered? How about our self-image? Are we ready to see ourselves as we are, in totality?

The Age of Belief for the past two thousand years has been an age of images which became the vehicles for direct experience. These images were hidden and presented in myths, allegories, and fairy tales. Later, the rational mind took over control and tried to make images into truths, instead of vehicles of the truth. The rational mind "puts on the brakes" and when growth, movement, and change stop, there is death. Thus, fundamental doctrines are born. The rational mind has said that it wants to know, but only if the knowing supports its fundamental beliefs. That is why there are very few scientists in any age who are willing to go beyond what their community states is true.

To say we are ready to move into the "New Age" is one thing; to be prepared to take responsibility for it is another. It is the Cosmic Warrior who makes this step, for this movement is not from the head but from the gut. Will you make that step or cling to the rhetoric, promises, and dogmas of the past? The movement into the "New Age" is not taking place because the old age was wrong. It is only natural that this unfolding continues. Nature's chant is "neti, neti, neti"—it is neither this nor that. The "New Age" is just another perspective on the wholeness already present. What makes it and every moment special is *you*, your *awareness*.

In the "New Age", it will be more difficult to hide behind images. Naturally, the rational mind will attempt to conquer and control but it will be left with a feeling of "something missing."

The Cosmic Warrior is born into new awareness. As a "Life Messenger," he is one who reveals life *by being*.

Those who try to sell this "life" and its belief to us are "death merchants." Their attempt is to sell the idea that life, reality, and God are outside us. Whatever the age, the message is the same: Life.

How can we get something we already have? Our attempts to achieve higher consciousness block the self-awareness already present. Is your life direction based on theory (either yours or others')? Do you live in timelessness? Will this "New Age" offer new plans on how to forget?

It is during times of change that we find ourselves between major systems. We are no longer in the past, yet the "New Age" has not yet emerged. It is during moments such as these that we are actually closer to who we are. We no longer find ourselves rooted in past belief patterns, yet we are not fully understanding the depth and dimension of the "New Age."

We find ourselves today in the in-between where the past no longer fits, and the so-called future is not ready for us. The truth that nothing gives identity is easier to see at this moment, because we are not receiving feedback on who we are in the midst of all the change. Embrace this time of transition, for it is in-between you will see yourself. This is the meditative moment on the macrocosmic scale.

In modern times a great deal of nonsense is talked about masters and disciples, and about the inheritance of a master's teaching by favorite pupils, entitling them to pass the truth on to their adherents. Of course Zen should be imparted in this way, from heart to heart, and in the past it was really accomplished. Silence and humility reigned rather than profession and assertion. The one who received such a teaching kept the matter hidden even after twenty years. Not until another discovered through his own need that a real master was at hand was it learned that the teaching had been imparted, and even then the occasion arose quite naturally and the teaching made its way in its own right. Under no circumstance did the teacher even claim "I am the successor of So-and-so." Such a claim would prove quite the contrary.

The Zen master Mu-nan had only one successor. His name was Shoju. After Shoju had completed his study of Zen, Mu-nan called him into his room. "I am getting old," he said, "and as far as I know, Shoju, you are the only one who will carry on this teaching. Here is a book. It has been passed down from master to master for seven generations. I also have added many points according to my understanding. The book is very valuable, and I am giving it to you to represent your successorship."

"If the book is such an important thing, you had better keep it," Shoju replied. "I received your Zen without writing and am satisfied with it as it is."

"I know that," said Mu-nan. "Even so, this work has been carried from master to master for seven generations, so you may keep it as a symbol of having received the teaching. Here.''

The two happened to be talking before a brazier. The instant Shoju felt the book in his hands he thrust it into the flaming coals. He had no lust for possessions.

Mu-nan, who never had been angry before, yelled: ''What are you doing!''

Shoju shouted back: ''What are you saying!''

—*Zen Flesh, Zen Bones**

**Zen Flesh, Zen Bones* by Paul Reps. Quoted by permission of Charles E. Tuttle Co., Inc., of Tokyo, Japan.

About the Author

MY FIRST ENCOUNTER WITH John Flint came about as the result of a 'book experience.' I had read the book, *Autobiography of a Yogi* by Yogananda and was curious to know more about the science of Kriya Yoga, one of the chapters in the book. For many months I searched for someone who could tell me more about Kriya Yoga. Finally, I read that a person named John Warren Flint, whose spiritual name was Swami Kriya-Dharmananda, was in Houston giving a lecture. Surely, he would be able to tell me something about Kriya; after all, it was a part of his name!

And now I find myself once again connected with John Flint through another 'book experience.' I have been asked to tell you about him as the author of his first book. Like all of us, John wears many 'hats,'—husband, father, step-father, son, brother, volunteer fireman, counselor and astrologer. He wears all of these well, but these are just images and do not tell you about the person inside.

John is a Life Messenger dreaming a magnificent dream he wants to share with all. His journey in this life began in a small suburb north of Chicago, continued at Purdue Univeristy in Indiana where he experienced his rebirth as a Life Messenger. From there he lived and studied in Boulder, Colorado, and back to Chicago, where he spent three years studying at a Hindu Temple. In 1974 he incorporated the Life Messenger Foundation, a non-profit organization.

Professionally, John is a gifted and intuitive astrologer, and personally John is my beloved. I am eager for you to share his dream as it is presented in this book.

Bari

Books I Have Enjoyed
Reading and Digesting

Autobiography of a Yogi, Yogananda

Zen Mind Beginners Mind, Suzuki

Zen Flesh Zen Bones, Reps

Various books by Rajneesh

The Transit of Saturn, Marc Robertson

Love is Letting Go of Fear, Jampolsky

Handbook to Higher Consciousness, Keyes

Stranger in a Strange Land, Heinlein

Illusions, Bach

The Tao Te Ching

Cosmic-view, The Universe in 40 Jumps, Boeke

Dhammapada

The Stand, and other Stephen King books

Astrology, Psychology and the Four Elements, Arroyo

The Crystal Cave Trilogy, Stewart

Tappan on Survival, Tappan

The Little Prince, de Saint-Exupery